Dedicated
to all of the
Reds that have
touched
our lives

Loss through my eyes

Birth – 2 years

I don't know what is happening, but I can see that people in my family are upset. Everyone seems very busy and my daily schedule has changed. With all of these emotions and changes in routine I might get a little fussy.

You can help me by trying to maintain my schedule. Someone might need to help, but having a sense of normalcy in this stressful time helps me feel secure.

2 – 4 years

I have a hard time understanding that my loved one isn't coming back. The future is hard for me to think about. I respond to my present needs and concerns. With my focus on the present my emotional responses can be brief, but intense.

You can help me by providing simple, honest answers to my questions as they arise. I also need frequent assurances, this helps me feel loved and supported.

4 - 7 years

To me the world is a magical place and I am at the center of it. I may feel guilty for the loss because I think I did something wrong. I am still trying to understand the future and may have difficulty thinking my loved one is permanently gone. I like to ask questions so I'm sure I'll ask them all and probably more than once.

You can help me by assuring me the loss isn't my fault. Simple and honest answers to my many questions are best. I might ask the same questions many times so consistency is important. Expressing my emotions verbally is difficult for me to do. Try letting me draw, play, or act exactly how I feel. I may not seem sad all the time and I may not cry, but it doesn't mean that I'm not emotionally affected by the loss.

7 - 12 years

I am starting to understand the finality of the loss. I am learning many things in school. I like to ask very specific questions as I process through the loss. As I attempt to gain understanding I look to the world around me. I am curious about how others feel and if the way I feel is right.

You can help me by answering my questions and encouraging me to share my emotions. At times I might be open to talk, but other times I may not. It is important to give me options to help me maintain my sense of control. It helps to hear my emotions are normal and its ok to feel the way I do.

You're my favorite Fred.
And you're mine Red.

I've known you since you were little.
And you're all that I can remember.

We've had lots of fun,
like sledding down that big hill.
It was scary on top,
but you kept me safe.

And there was that time
we built a snowman.
He was so cool!
You helped with the hat
so I wouldn't need a stool.

We make a great team!
Forever Fred and Red!
I have to tell you Fred,
I have been feeling very sick.

You're such a great help, but I'm still very sick. I've tried many things, but my body still isn't working. Someday I won't be here anymore.

Where will you go?
Will it be like a vacation?
Can I come too?

It's not like a vacation and you can't come with me. It's a beautiful place for things that can't be fixed, but once I'm there I can't come back.

Of course I love you and
no matter what
I always will!

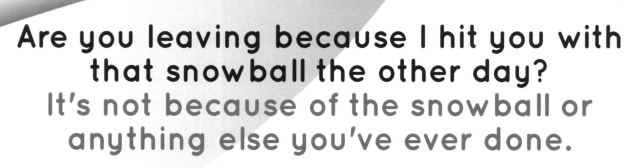

Are you leaving because I hit you with that snowball the other day?
It's not because of the snowball or anything else you've ever done.

**Well I don't believe you.
You'll get better then you
can stay forever!**

I know it's scary and hard to believe.
I wish I could stay.

THIS IS NOT FAIR!!!

I know it's not fair
and it's ok to be mad.
It helps to let the
anger out. Try jumping up and
down or drawing how you feel.

What if I shovel the snow?
Do you still have to go?
I'll even clean the igloo
if it means I always get to keep you!

That is very kind, but there is nothing
you can do. No matter how hard
you try, someday I won't
be here anymore.

It makes me so sad thinking
about life without you.
All I want to do is cry.

Like dress up!

And hide and seek even though you peek!

Don't forget

our painting!

I feel a little better now, but then sometimes I don't. I wish that you could stay forever. At least I'll always have our memories!

Lets make one more
memory before you go.
How about that hill?
One last time down the snow!

WAHOO!!!

This time on top
I wasn't even scared!
I couldn't be more proud my dear
little Fred.

I'm going to miss you!
I'll miss you too, but never forget
you'll always be my
sweet little Fred!

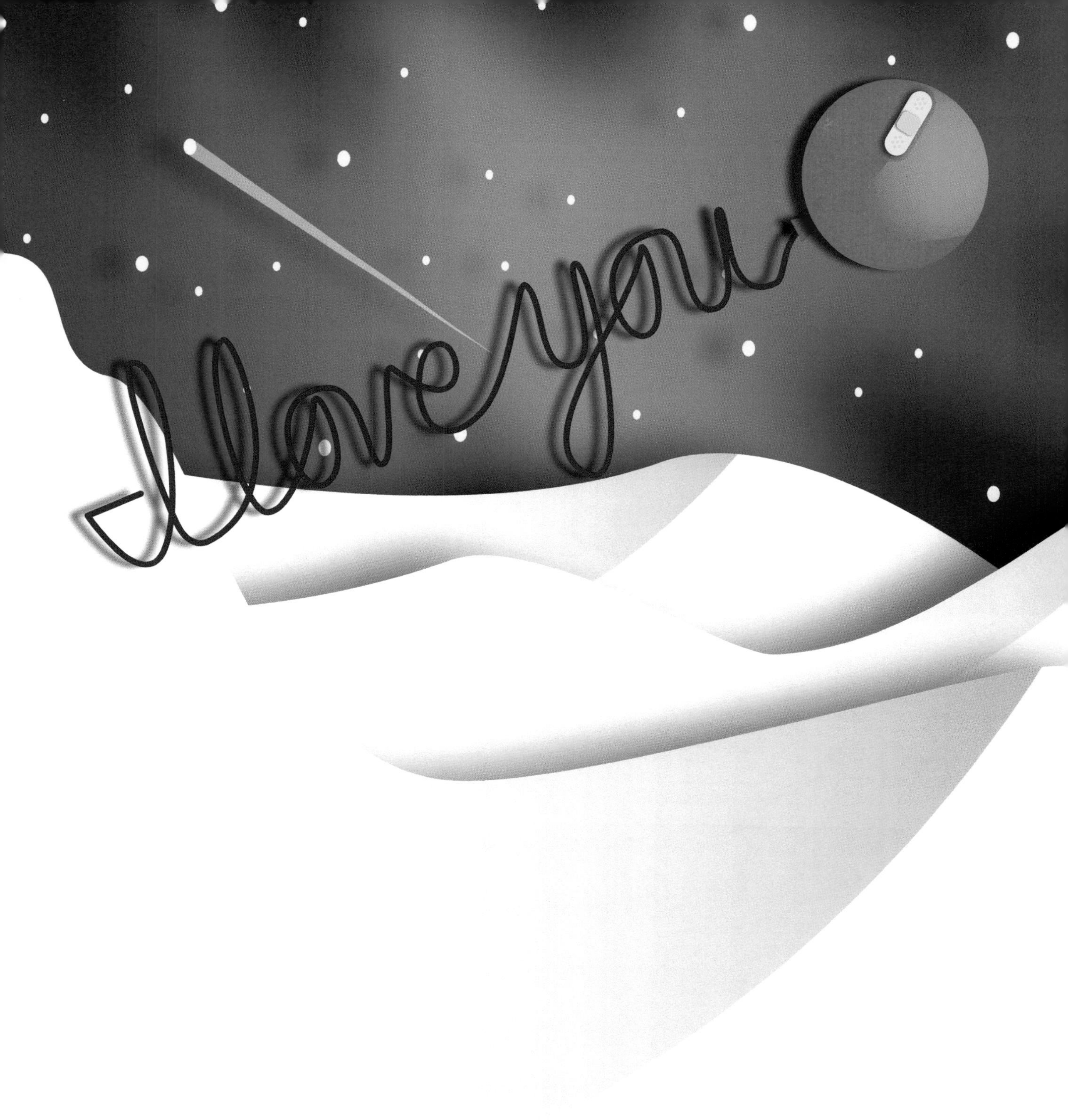
I love you

Proof

49662582R00019